ii

U.S. REGIONAL STRATEGY FOR NORTH KOREA

North Korea is one of the world's last holdovers from the Cold War era. Ruled by a hereditary autocrat, this harsh police-state is surrounded by large global economies in Japan, South Korea, and China, and yet by choice, it remains a poor and backwards nation that continues to spend 31.3% of its meager Gross Domestic Product (GDP) on weapons of mass destruction and its military.[1] North Korea has stood against the United States since the end of the Korean War in 1953, routinely spouting bellicose statements and making threats against successive U.S. administrations and American allies in the region. North Korea's seemingly erratic behavior and lack of basic freedoms and human rights are puzzling and an abomination to the democratic countries of the world.

The United States as the world's sole super-power is vastly superior to any other competitor in military capability and economic wealth. During the Korean War, the U.S. led the United Nation's effort to first push back the invading forces from North Korea and later its Chinese allies. This action resulted in American losses of 33,000 killed and 101,000 wounded. Since the end of the conflict, the U.S. has maintained forces in South Korea to prevent a renewed attempt by the North Koreans to reunify the peninsula by force.[2]

Today, the Korean Peninsula remains a divided and dangerous place. Large conventional military forces exist on both sides of the Demilitarized Zone (DMZ) and North Korea's missiles and Weapons of Mass Destruction (WMD) are a threat to not only South Korea but Japan and other countries in the region.[3] Today, the United States is no closer to normalizing relations with North Korea than in 1953. Unfortunately for the United States, the stakes are now much higher. The problem is no longer simply containing communism. North Korea's suspected nuclear weapons programs and other threats make the situation on the peninsula much deadlier with dire long-term consequences.

The Korean Peninsula is a volatile flashpoint because the United States has failed to implement a regional strategy for dealing with North Korea that goes far enough in guaranteeing lasting peace and stability in the region. President George W. Bush named North Korea a member of the "Axis of Evil" because of its suspected nuclear weapons programs, possession of ballistic missiles, proliferation of missile technology and ownership of other Weapons of Mass Destruction (WMD).[4] The President's declaration only exacerbated an already tense and distrustful relationship between the two countries.

The Bush Administration's current policy on North Korea consists of the following major themes:

1

- Terminating the 1994 Agreed Framework.[5]
- No negotiations with the North Koreans until it ends its nuclear weapons programs.[6]
- Establishing an international coalition to put economic pressure on the North Koreans.[7]
- Plans for the future use of economic sanctions and military force against North Korea.[8]
- Warnings to North Korea not to reprocess spent nuclear fuel rods for weapons grade plutonium.[9]

This policy has not yielded positive results and an impasse exists with North Korea over its nuclear weapons program. So far, the United States has refused to engage in bi-lateral negotiations with the North Koreans. Six-party talks aimed at creating a solution to this problem have thus far failed to yield any major breakthroughs. Renewed conflict on the Korean Peninsula would have a tremendously destabilizing effect on Northeast Asia, inflicting thousands of casualties in both Koreas and disrupting the economies of the region.

The September 11, 2001 terrorist attacks committed the United States to a Global War on Terrorism (GWOT) with ongoing combat and stabilization operations in Iraq and Afghanistan. The attacks caused the U.S. to change its policy for dealing with potential enemies. The current United States National Security Strategy, developed after September 11th 2001, calls for preemptive use of force to defeat rogue states that can threaten its security:

> The United States has long maintained the option of preemptive actions to counter a sufficient threat to our national security. The greater the threat, the greater is the risk of inaction – and the more compelling the case for taking anticipatory action to defend ourselves, even if uncertainty remains as to the time and place of the enemy's attack. To forestall or prevent such hostile acts by our adversaries, the United States will, if necessary, act preemptively.[10]

This policy of preemptive military action has created some difficult issues for the United States. Does the U.S. now strike first in all cases? Does the U.S. give up on engagement and negotiation? What does the United States do when its military means are over-committed and it is much more difficult and risky to use pre-emptive force? The answer to these questions is that the U.S. must use all of its elements of national power to attain its objectives and achieve the desired security for the nation. In the case of North Korea, it is time for the United States and North Korea to finally bring this conflict and fifty plus years of hostility to an end.

2

The United State's current North Korea policy has worsened the situation because it fails to effectively use all the elements of national power. Too much emphasis is placed on deterrence, isolation, punitive measures, and places the requirements for first steps on the North Koreans. The current administration views direct negotiations as a "reward" and not a crucial beginning for solving the North Korean situation. The United States must use bi-lateral as well as multi-national negotiations and engagement as an integral part of its strategy to achieve lasting stability on the Korean Peninsula.

SHAPING CURRENT POSITIONS

North Korea's relationship with the United States since 1953 can be characterized as hostile with plenty of mutual distrust. Both Koreas were devastated by the Korean War, a conflict that started with the North Korean invasion of South Korea.[11] After the end of that conflict, the United States committed itself to the mutual defense of South Korea and supplied that country with substantial military and economic aid. U.S. forces have remained in South Korea since 1953 and currently number around 30,000.

After the Korean War, North Korea continued to receive military and economic assistance from the Soviet Union and China. However, the collapse of the Soviet Union ended much of this aid and assistance. The impact on the North Korean economy was tremendously adverse and it has never recovered.[12] North Korea has long viewed the government in South Korea as a puppet for the United States and the U.S. forces stationed in South Korea as a potential invasion force.

The decades following the Korean War were marked by a series of incidents with the North Koreans. In January 1968, the USS Pueblo, a U.S. Navy reconnaissance ship was captured by North Korean forces in international waters in the Sea of Japan.[13] This, and the 1970's tree-cutting incident along the DMZ are two of the better known clashes which have occurred over the past 50-years . More recently, North Korean aircraft intercepted a U.S. RC-135 reconnaissance plane in international airspace over the Sea of Japan on March 2, 2003 and tried to force it down.[14]

The current U.S. policy on North Korea reflects the George W. Bush Administration's distrust of the Kim, Jong- II regime and repudiation of the "engagement and enlargement" policies employed by the Clinton Administration. The Clinton strategy was perceived as being too soft on the North Koreans. In an effort to halt North Korea's nuclear weapons program, the Clinton Administration offered energy aid and the promise of normalized relations to the North Koreans. After winning the 2000 elections, the Bush Administration reviewed the Clinton policy

3

and reversed itself on this approach. United States support to North Korea under the 1994 Agreed Framework, consisting of energy aid and construction of two nuclear reactors, was suspended.[15] In August 2003, the United States along with China, Russia, Japan, and South Korea began six-party talks in an attempt to solve the North Korean Nuclear issue.[16] Talks are currently stalled and there is little progress to show for this effort.

While some aspects of the current North Korean strategy are valid, the overall strategy is not balanced when compared against all the available elements of national power. More weight is given to military and hard-line options than others that are available. Vice President Cheney summed up U.S. policy on North Korea when he stated "we don't negotiate with evil, we defeat it."[17] This approach has done more to provoke North Korea than solve the issue as evidenced by the following:

- In October 2002, the United States alleges that the North Koreans have a secret uranium enrichment program.[18]
- In December 2002, North Korea expels inspectors from the United Nation's International Atomic Energy Agency and later withdraws from the Nuclear Nonproliferation Treaty.[19]
- In March 2003, in response to the U.S. refusal to hold bi-lateral talks, the North Koreans test fired a missile into the Sea of Japan (East Sea).[20]
- In October 2003, the North Koreans announced that 8,000 spent nuclear fuel rods were re-processed for weapons grade plutonium.[21]
- In November 2003, North Korean energy aid and the construction of two light water nuclear reactors under the 1994 Agreed Framework were suspended.[22]
- In 2004, revelations surfaced that South Korea conducted its own nuclear experiments in 1982 and 2000.[23]

These events do not reflect a successful strategy. In fact, they demonstrate that the current U.S. policy is doing little to bring stability to the Korean Peninsula and is in fact raising tensions instead of reducing them. The current strategy is unsuccessful because it fails to use *direct* engagement, either diplomatic or economic, as a method to *induce* North Korea to change its behavior. Given the current situation there, there is little doubt that a new strategy is needed.

4

WHY A NEW STRATEGY IS NEEDED

The Korean Peninsula has the misfortune of being located between Northeast Asia's greatest powers – China and Japan. Historically, the Koreans have been dominated by both countries and colonized by the Japanese.[24] Korea is a strategic buffer in this very important part of the world. The U.S. presence in South Korea since the end of the Korean War has provided stability to the region by deterring further aggression by the North Koreans and creating a climate for the remarkable economic growth of both South Korea and Japan. These countries, both former monarchies in the last century, are now healthy democracies and our strongest allies in the region.

The current hard-line policy of the United States risks alienating Japan and South Korea. Both are actively engaging the North Koreans and are frustrated with the U.S. position of no bilateral negotiations.[25] The use of military force to effect regime change in North Korea would be catastrophic to the populace of South Korea especially given its vulnerability and proximity to North Korean conventional artillery.[26] The economies of Japan, as well as those of China and the United States would also be severely impacted. These countries are South Korea's three largest trading partners. The United States alone exported $24.4 billion in goods to South Korea in 2003 while importing $35 billion in South Korean products.[27]

A United States led regime change in North Korea could also prove very difficult given the ongoing commitments to operations in Iraq and Afghanistan. There is no doubt that the current strategy has not worked. It is time for the U.S. and the current administration to employ more than military power and political and economic isolation in its strategy if it wishes to bring long-term stability to the Korean Peninsula.

North Korea's nuclear weapons programs are the most serious threat to the region, but there is other North Korean behavior that threatens the stability of the Korean Peninsula and relations with the United States and its allies. The United States will have to address these threats in any future strategy for the region.

THREATS

North Korea threatens U.S. interests and regional stability with its WMD programs, large conventional military forces, ballistic missiles and long-range artillery, economic instability, refugee problems, and illicit drug trade. The intent of the Kim, Jong-Il regime is to stay in power at all costs. The North Korean leadership firmly believes that the United States is committed to using force to topple the regime. Operation Iraqi Freedom has only solidified the North Korean position and they will pursue all means, including nuclear weapons, to deter the United States from effecting a regime change.[28] North Korea's stated policy is the reunification of the Korean Peninsula under the communist banner. However, given the poor state of its economy, lack of energy stocks, and the outdated equipment of its conventional forces, it is questionable if North Korea could sustain a deliberate conventional attack on South Korea. A North Korean invasion of South Korea would be the last act of a desperate regime.[29]

WEAPONS OF MASS DESTRUCTION PROGRAMS

Under the 1994 Agreed Framework, the North Koreans agreed to freeze their plutonium-based nuclear weapons program in exchange for energy aid and the construction of two light-water nuclear reactors by a consortium consisting of the United States, Japan and South Korea (KEDO). The program was suspended after the U.S. presented evidence that the North Koreans possessed a secret uranium enrichment program.[30] At a minimum, the U.S. is fairly certain that the North Koreans possess some number of plutonium-based weapons and have the capability to produce more from plutonium obtained from reprocessed spent fuel rods from the Yongbyon nuclear reactor.[31]

It is also suspected that the North Koreans possess large quantities of chemical weapons and stocks of biological weapons and can produce substantial additional quantities of both. A major concern of the current U.S. Administration is the possibility of North Korean WMD sales to Al-Qaeda or other terrorist organizations.

CONVENTIONAL MILITARY FORCES AND BALLISTIC MISSILES

The North Korean armed forces number 1.2 million.[32] Its special operations forces are the largest in the world and number 120,000. The North Koreans also possess large quantities of artillery and submarines[33] and their long-range artillery can range Seoul from its current positions. Much of their equipment is outdated, but the sheer numbers make this force a very potent threat to South Korea and the U.S. forces stationed on the peninsula. Two-thirds of North Korean forces are stationed within close proximity of the DMZ with the potential to initiate offensive operations with little to no warning.[34]

It is suspected that the North Koreans have around 800 missiles of various types and ranges that can threaten not only South Korea but Japan and possibly portions of the United States and its territories.[35] The missiles pose an even greater danger if coupled with nuclear warheads or chemical and biological weapons.

REFUGEE PROBLEMS

The numbers of defectors from North Korea continues to rise. From 2001 to 2003, 3008 North Koreans have escaped and sought asylum in South Korea.[36] It is estimated that these numbers will continue to rise. Most defectors escape across the Chinese border and it is thought that 300,000 North Korean refugees are currently in China.[37] Large numbers of refugees threaten not only China's stability and economy but will stress South Korea's ability to absorb them into their society and economy over the long-run.

ECONOMIC INSTABILITY

The North Korean economy is in poor shape. Once Soviet aid and markets dried up, the state-run economic system quickly collapsed.[38] The North Koreans are experimenting with reforms and are exercising unprecedented freedoms in open markets vice the state monopolies of earlier years. Government subsidies for food and other products have ended. The North Koreans are also looking to attract foreign investment from South Korea and other countries. An attempt at a foreign partnership now has automobiles assembled and sold in North Korea using Fiat parts.[39]

If North Korea imploded today, South Korea would struggle with the enormous costs of absorbing the broken economy of the North.[40] When contrasted with German reunification, the economy and infrastructure of North Korea are in much worse shape than the former East Germany.

ILLICIT DRUG TRADE

In April 2003, a North Korean owned ship was boarded in Australia and 125 kilograms of heroin were found. The heroin was worth $144 million.[41] The United States and other countries have long suspected that the North Koreans are heavily involved in the illegal drug trade and that the trade is sponsored and encouraged by the North Korean government. It is estimated that the North Koreans produce 40-tons of opium a year and process the opium into heroin. This, combined with the manufacture of other illegal drugs, brings in an approximated $1 billion annually to the cash-poor country.[42] Much of the North Korean drugs are sold in Japan and it is also believed that the North Koreans have partnered with Russian and Japanese organized crime organizations to operate the drug trade.

REGIONAL ARMS RACE

North Korea's nuclear weapons program has the potential for sparking a regional arms race. In 2004, it was revealed that South Korea conducted its own experiments with nuclear materials in 1982 and 2000.[43] This occurred despite the fact that the United States had "convinced" the South Koreans to abandon their nuclear weapons programs in the late 1970's. Japan is now an active partner in the U.S missile defense initiative and is contemplating its own offensive missile capability.

North Korea poses a significant threat to the stability of the region. U.S. allies and other countries that are important to its interests are also threatened. Finding a resolution to the long-standing problems with North Korea is important to not only the United States but many other countries. It is vital that the U.S. utilize its allies and friends in the process of finding, formulating and executing a solution to the North Korean problem.

POTENTIAL ALLIES

Implementation of a successful regional strategy for North Korea will require the assistance of allies and other nations in the region. The six-party talks designed to convince North Korea to rid itself of its nuclear weapons programs is a good example of using allies to achieve a common objective. This approach could be a starting point for developing other multi-lateral mechanisms and agreements to deal with North Korea.

SOUTH KOREA

The country that stands to lose the most in the event that open hostilities resume on the Korean Peninsula is South Korea.[44] The South has made a remarkable recovery from the devastation of the Korean War and is now the world's twelfth largest economy. South Korea has a very active engagement program with the North Koreans that includes regular political and military talks as well as economic and emergency aid. The two countries now have many cultural and sports exchanges and routine reunions are held between family members separated during the Korean War.[45]

JAPAN

After South Korea, Japan is the next country most threatened by North Korea's ballistic missiles and other WMD. U.S. forces are stationed in Japan and Okinawa and the U.S. will use Japanese ports and facilities in the event of renewed conflict on the peninsula. Japan's colonial history on the Korean Peninsula and use of Korean citizens during World War II are a source of tension with both Koreas.[46] Japan has the world's second largest economy which could be severely disrupted by renewed hostilities on the Korean Peninsula. Over the years, North Korea has kidnapped Japanese citizens. The recent return and admission of the kidnappings by the North Koreans greatly angered the Japanese population.[47]

CHINA AND RUSSIA

Both of these countries are long-time allies of North Korea and both countries have provided military and economic aid over the years. Renewed conflict in Korea could hinder China's booming economic growth and its significant trade ties with the U.S., Japan and South Korea. China continues to provide North Korea with energy and food aid and there is significant trade between the two countries along their shared border.[48] Russia and China are active partners in the ongoing six-party talks to end North Korea's nuclear programs.[49]

EUROPE

The European Union is another potential partner for creating a stable Northeast Asia. Countries of the European Union are actively engaged with North Korea and could play an important role in creating solutions for the many problems of the region.[50]

THE UNITED NATIONS

While not a formal ally, any successful solution to the North Korea problem will require the assistance of the United Nations. The International Atomic Energy Agency (IAEA) is needed to verify compliance with nuclear disarmament requirements. The World Bank and International Monetary Fund could also be used to provide economic and monetary assistance to North Korea.

OPPORTUNITIES

A successful U.S. strategy for North Korea has the potential to create the conditions for lasting stability in the region. A stable Korean Peninsula would create an environment conducive to the peaceful reunification of the two Koreas. Peace and stability would also allow North Korea to reform its economy and end the long years of food and energy shortages. A breakthrough in the current situation would also enable the country to participate in the process of globalization and at long last cast off its self-imposed isolation and secretiveness. There is also an opportunity to free up the U.S. forces stationed in South Korea and Japan for other worldwide missions, particularly the ongoing GWOT.

ENGAGEMENT – OTHER EXAMPLES AND LESSONS LEARNED

Active engagement and dialog must be used to normalize relations between the United States and North Korea. During the Clinton Administration, engagement was used in an attempt to end North Korea's nuclear weapons ambitions. There are lessons from the Clinton approach that can be used in a future U.S. policy.

ENGAGEMENT - THE CLINTON APPROACH

After contemplating a military solution and finding it unacceptable, the Clinton Administration opted to use active engagement with the North Koreans. This approach resulted in the Agreed Framework of 1994. Under this agreement, North Korea was rewarded with energy aid, the construction of two "proliferation resistant," light-water nuclear reactors and the prospect of normalized relations with the U.S. In return, the North Koreans "promised" to freeze their plutonium-based weapons program.[51] The U.S. Secretary of State traveled to North Korea and met with North Korean representatives including Kim, Jong Il. The Clinton strategy seemed successful and it appeared as if the United States and North Korea were headed toward a peaceful resolution to the nuclear weapons crisis and possibly normalized relations.

Unfortunately, the Clinton approach had some flaws. First, the North Koreans were allowed to retain spent fuel rods from their Yongbyon nuclear power facility. It is now suspected that the North Koreans have reprocessed these rods and extracted weapons-grade plutonium to build additional nuclear weapons. The 1994 Agreed Framework contained no prohibitions for weapons programs based on uranium enrichment nor did it require the removal of spent fuel rods from North Korea prior to receiving energy aid.[52] The agreement also lacked any strong verification mechanisms. The North Koreas were allowed to constrain the inspection routines and access of United Nations inspectors.

The Clinton Administration's engagement efforts with North Korea were not perfect and ultimately failed to achieve the desired results. However, it should not mean that the United States rules out active engagement as an option. New U.S. engagement efforts must include mechanisms to ensure compliance with agreements and be tied to quid-pro-quo actions by both parties.

ENGAGEMENT – SOUTH KOREA AND EUROPE

Probably the most active engagement policy currently underway is that of the South Koreans. The "Sunshine Policy" was initiated by President Kim, Dae Jung in an effort to normalize relations between the two Koreas and set the conditions for an eventual peaceful reunification.[53] This comprehensive program includes South Korean economic investment in North Korea, the opening of transportation corridors through the Demilitarized Zone, sports and cultural exchanges, and the first ever military-to military talks in 2004.[54] It is a vital interest of South Korea to pursue a policy of engagement. Military conflict on the Korean Peninsula would be bloody and devastate the economy and infrastructure of South Korea.[55] If North Korea collapses on its own, South Korea would inherit the North's non-existent economy and all the "ills" that come with a society brutalized by a repressive regime. The economic burden on South Korea to absorb the North would be crushing. Additionally, China is fearful of a large influx of North Korean refugees fleeing a collapsing country. [56]

Several European countries are also working hard to engage and normalize relations with North Korea. Germany has established a western cultural center in North Korea's capital Pyongyang and the North Koreans are assembling there own automobiles using Fiat parts from Italy. Britain and Australia have established diplomatic relations with the North Koreans. Japan's prime minister has made two visits to North Korea and seems intent on normalizing relations.[57]

South Korea, Britain, Japan and others believe that engagement and support for North Korea's efforts to transform its economy will modify their behavior and induce them to give up their WMD programs.[58] The Clinton version of engagement with North Korea, while not perfect, did get the North Koreans to the table. A case can be made that it was successful in getting the North Koreans to freeze their plutonium-based weapons program until the current administration stopped the energy aid promised under the 1994 Agreed Framework.

The current North Korea strategy of the Bush Administration does not include direct talks or active engagement. In fact, the administration has thus far refused to consider or accept bi-lateral discussions with North Korea. It is time to realize that the prospects for normalizing and stabilizing the region will remain low unless engagement is included in the strategy.

PROPOSED STRATEGY

The United States must revise its current approach to North Korea if it intends to solve not only the ongoing nuclear impasse but also bring a long overdue end to the conflict of the Korean War. A proposed strategy for North Korea must include all elements of national power. Bi-lateral talks, direct engagement, as well as the threat of all forms of punitive action must be included.

The objectives or ends for this proposed strategy include:

ENDS
- A Korean Peninsula free of nuclear weapons.
- Reduced conventional military forces in North and South Korea.
- A stable Korean Peninsula, with conditions set for eventual peaceful reunification.
- North Korean missile programs dismantled.
- Improved human rights conditions in North Korea.

The methods for accomplishing these ends are:

WAYS

- Bi-lateral talks and political engagement with the intent of normalizing U.S./North Korean relations.
- Aid and assistance to modernize and create growth in the North Korean economy.
- Energy assistance.
- Additional reductions in U.S. ground forces stationed in South Korea linked to Quid-pro-quo reductions and re-stationing of North Korean ground forces.
- Support political and economic engagement efforts by South Korea, Japan, and the European Union.
- Utilize Non-Governmental Organizations to educate the North Korean leadership and populace on human rights.

The resources or means for implementing and accomplishing this strategy in decreasing priority are:

MEANS

- Economic and energy aid.
- Diplomacy.
- Sanctions.
- Military action.

ANALYSIS OF PROPOSED STRATEGY

This proposed strategy retains some aspects of the current U.S. policy and adds direct engagement and bi-lateral talks with the North Koreans. The ends include objectives for removing the North Korean threats of nuclear weapons and ballistic missile programs as well as setting the conditions for eventual reunification between the two Koreas. The centerpiece of this strategy is the use of a quid-pro-quo methodology. Positive actions by the North Koreans are reciprocated with rewards. This "carrot and stick" approach is more likely to produce the desired policy objectives. The recent breakthrough with Libya is a successful example of using engagement to induce a country to give up its WMD programs.[59]

This proposed strategy is a dramatic change from the hard-line, no-direct negotiations stance of the current U.S. policy. The threat of U.S. pre-emptive force, as stated in the current National Security Strategy, should only be used in the event that no progress is made with direct

12

engagement. Renewed military conflict on the Korean Peninsula would be extremely bloody and would be the direct result of failed diplomacy, imagination and cooperation.

The methods or ways of this regional policy are feasible and would compliment the ongoing engagement efforts of South Korea and others. In other words, the U.S would not carry the burden alone. The reliance on quid-pro-quo responses from the North Koreans ensures that rewards of aid and normalized relations are only given if the North Koreans follow through with positive and verifiable actions.

Choosing to use direct negotiations, the United States can be certain that North Korea clearly understands its position on the issues. It could remove some of the suspicion and doubt that North Korea has concerning U.S. intentions. It also provides an opportunity for the U.S. to convey to the North that engagement and rewards come at a cost – positive actions on their part and that the U.S. has not ruled out the use of punitive measures in the event that progress stalls.

RISKS

This proposed strategy of engagement and direct negotiation involves risks that would have to be monitored and addressed:

LACK OF VERIFICATION

In order for this strategy to succeed there must be a legitimate process to verify North Korean compliance. As stated earlier, the 1994 Agreed Framework failed because it did not have full-proof verification mechanisms. For this plan to be successful, there must be a better system. No concessions or aid should be given until it can be verified that the North Koreans have taken concrete steps to dismantle their WMD programs or reduce conventional forces. The United Nations, IAEA is probably the only acceptable organization for this task.

DISFUNCTIONAL MULTINATIONAL EFFORT

A lasting settlement of the North Korean problem will require the support and assistance of many nations. Like the ongoing six-party talks, it may prove difficult to get all partners moving in the same direction at all times. Significant differences in opinion and interests could derail the process. The assistance and cooperation of other countries is necessary for this strategy to succeed and the U.S. will have to work very hard to achieve consensus. The U.S. can not bear the entire burden of providing economic and energy assistance to the North Koreans.

USE OF MILITARY FORCE

If the North Koreans renege on agreements or refuse to comply, there must be a credible threat of military force to gain compliance. However, despite our existing alliance with South Korea it may be very difficult to get agreement from them on the use of pre-emptive military force. South Korea has invested much effort and resources in its engagement efforts with the North and would also take the full brunt of any North Korean retaliatory strikes. This reluctance could cause a rift between the United States and South Korea.

ISOLATION

Similar to the use of military force, a united effort to further isolate North Korea may be difficult to achieve given the various interests of our friends and allies in the region. This could make the implementation of trade sanctions and embargoes ineffective and disjointed.

The greatest risk is that the United States continues its current hard-line approach and does not utilize some form of direct negotiations and engagement to end the current impasse with North Korea.

RECOMMENDATIONS

The United States must adopt an approach that is similar to this outlined strategy if it desires a peaceful settlement to the North Korean issue. Direct engagement, to include bi-lateral talks and negotiations stand a better chance of producing results. The hard-line approach currently being used by the Bush Administration is not working and conditions on the Korean Peninsula are worse than when President Bush took office in 2001. Due to existing commitments to the GWOT in Iraq and Afghanistan, it would be extremely difficult for the United States to use military force to effect a regime change in North Korea. South Korea, a close ally, is committed to trying other options before using preemptive military force.[60] Strikes on North Korean WMD production and delivery systems would likely elicit a retaliatory response from the North Koreans that could escalate the situation on the Korean Peninsula into open war. The cost in lives and the destruction to South Korea would be devastating. United States forces stationed in South Korea would also be exposed to a North Korean military response. The "best" option is for the United States to utilize the full range of tools that are part of its national power to end its long history of conflict with the North Koreans.

CONCLUSION

The current United States policy on North Korea fails to use all the elements of national power. A comprehensive strategy that incorporates active engagement, bi-lateral negotiations, multi-national cooperation, and includes strong mechanisms for verification should be implemented. However, it must also include the threat of military force or further political and economic isolation for non-compliance if measurable progress is not achieved.

United States participation in the six-party talks is a good *starting point*. It must now build and expand on this effort. The U.S. should not and cannot be the sole contributor to finding a solution to this very difficult problem. But, this does not mean that any options, to include direct dialog and active engagement should be discounted. The U.S. must adopt this new approach if it is truly serious about improving and normalizing relations with North Korea and bringing to an end 53-years and counting of conflict and hostility.

WORD COUNT=5551

ENDNOTES

[1]"North and South Korean Military Comparisons 2002"; available from <http://www.paulnoll.com/Korea/History/Korean-military.html>; Internet; accessed 26 September 2004.

[2]Larry A. Niksch, "Korea: U.S.- Korean Relations Issues for Congress," CRS Issue Brief for Congress, 18 July 2003, p. CRS-1; available from <http://fas.org/man/crs/IB98045.pdf>; Internet; accessed 18 January 2005.

[3]"Committee on International Relations – Congressional Testimony," U.S. House of Representatives, 24 September 1998, p. 9; available from <http://commdocs.house.gov/committees/intrel/hfa52334.000/hfa52334_0.htm>; Internet; accessed 29 August 2004.

[4]The Friends Committee on National Legislation (FCNL), "U.S. Policy towards North Korea: An Overview," August 2003, p.1; available from <http://www.fcnl.org/whatis.htm>; Internet; accessed 29 August 2004.

[5]Larry A. Niksch, "Korea: U.S.- Korean Relations Issues for Congress, Summary," CRS Issue Brief for Congress, 18 July 2003, p. 07-18-03; available from <http://fas.org/man/crs/IB98045.pdf>; Internet; accessed 18 January 2005.

[6]Ibid.

[7]Ibid.

[8]Ibid.

[9]Ibid.

[10]George W. Bush, *The National Security Strategy of the United States of America* (Washington D.C.: The White House, September 2002), p. 15.

[11]Bernard Brodie, *TheTest of Korea, War and Politics,* (New York: Macmillian Publishing Co, 1973), p. 106.

[12]Defense Intelligence Agency, "North Korea: The Foundations of Military Strength," October 1991, p. 4; available from <http://www.fas.org/irp/product/knfms/knfms_chp3.html>; Internet; accessed 19 December 2004.

[13]"U.S.S. Pueblo Exhibit, National Security Agency Museum, Exhibit Summary"; available from <http://www.nsa.gov/museum/museu00032.cfm>; Internet ; accessed 8 December 2004.

[14]Kathleen T. Rhem, "North Korea Intercepts Air Force Aircraft," *Air Force Print News*, American Forces Print Service, March 2003; available from <http://www.af.mil/news/story_print.asp?storyID=30403665>; Internet; accessed 8 December 2004.

[15]David E. Sanger, "U.S. Persuades Allies to Halt North Korean Atom Project," *New York Times*, (June 2004); [database on-line]; available from ProQuest; accessed 31 August 2004.

[16]Graham Allison, " '94 Deal With North Korea Holds Lessons for Today," *New York Times*, p. E-6 (July 2004); [database on-line]; available from ProQuest; accessed 31 August 2004.

[17]"Country Watch. North Korea – 2004 Country Review, Country Watch Reviews ," 2004 ed., p.17; available from <http://www.countrywatch.com>; Internet; accessed 8 August 2004.

[18]"Six Party Talks, U.S. Department of State Press Release," 2 March 2004; available from <http://www.state.gov/p/eap/rls/rm/2004/30093.htm>; Internet; accessed 23 January 2005.

[19]"Country Watch, North Korea, p.18-19."

[20]Ibid., 20

[21]Ibid., 22

[22]Ibid., 17

[23]"North Korea Won't abandon Nuclear Programs, North Korea Says It Can't Abandon Nuclear programs After South Korean Nuclear Experiments," *The Associated Press*, September 2004, ABCNews.com; available from <http://printerfriendly.abcnews.com/ printerfriendly/Print?fetchFromGLUE=true&GLUESer>; Internet; accessed 5 October 2004.

[24]"Country Watch, North Korea, p.7."

[25] Gordon Fairclough, "Seoul Steps up Push for Dealing with Pyongyang; South Korea Will Urge U.S. to Be More Flexible in Nuclear Program Talks ," *Wall Street Journal*, p. A10 (31 August 2004); [database on-line]; available from ProQuest; accessed 8 September 2004.

[26]Marcus Noland, "North Korea and the South Korean Economy," Institute for International Economics, 24 February 2003, p.1; available from <http://www.iie.com/publications/papers/ noland0203.htm>; Internet; accessed 23 January 2005.

[27]The Central Intelligence Agency, "The World Factbook, South Korea," 2003, p. 7-8; available from <http://www.cia.gov/cia/publications/factbook/print/ks.html>; Internet; accessed 23 January 2005.

[28]Strategic Asia 2003-04, *Fragility & Crisis*, (Seattle: The National Bureau of Asian Research), p.144.

[29]Ibid., 132.

[30]"Country Watch, North Korea, 17."

[31]Ibid., 22.

[32]"Country Watch, North Korea, 35."

[33]Kathleen Rhem, "North Korean Military Very Credible Conventional Force ," United States Department of Defense, American Forces Information Service News Articles, November 2003;

available from <http://www.defenselink.mil/news/Nov2003/n11182003_200311181.html>; Internet; accessed 15 September 2004.

[34]Ibid.

[35]Ibid.

[36]Gregg Chenowith and Tricia Miller, "A Heartless Homeland," *Christianity Today*, October 2004; available from <http://www.christianitytoday.com/ct/2004/010/29.45.html>; Internet; accessed 26 October 2004.

[37]Ibid.

[38]James Brooke, "2 Koreas Sidestep U.S. to Forge Pragmatic Links ." *The New York Times*, p. A2 (26 June 2004); [database on-line]; available from ProQuest; accessed 31 August 2004.

[39]Norimitsu Onishi, "North Korea Is Reaching Out and World Is Reaching Back," *The New York Times*, p. A.1 (August 2004); [database on-line]; available from ProQuest; accessed 8 September 2004.

[40]Brooke, A1.

[41]An-Young Kim, "Targeting Pyongyang's Drug Trade Addiction," Asia Times – Online, June 2003; available from <http://www.atimes.com/atimes/Korea/EF18Dg02.html>; Internet; accessed 7 November 2004.

[42]Ibid.

[43]"North Korea Won't abandon Nuclear Programs, North Korea Says It Can't Abandon Nuclear programs After South Korean Nuclear Experiments."

[44]Brooke, A1.

[45]Ibid.

[46]"Country Watch, North Korea, 7."

[47]James Brooke, "Japanese Angry Over Korean Kidnappings ," *The New York Times*, 20 March 2002; available from <http://www.freeserbia.net/Articles/2002/Kidnappings.html>; Internet; accessed 19 December 2004.

[48]"On China's Aid to North Korea and Sanctions," ParaPundit, 9 July 2003; available from <http://www.parapundit.com/archives/001464.html>; Internet; accessed 19 December 2004.

[49]Richard Boucher, Spokesman, U.S. Department of State – Press Statement, "Six-Party Talks on North Korean Nuclear Program," 28 February 2004; available from <http://www.state.gov/r/pa/prs/ps/2004/29989.htm>; Internet; accessed 19 December 2004.

[50]Onishi, A1.

[51]Paul Kerr, *"U.S. Unveils Offer at North Korea Talks,"* *Arms Control Today*, July/August 2004, p.36.

[52]James A. Baker, "Nuclear Pyongyang," *The Wall Street Journal*, p. A.12 (August 2004); [database on-line]; available from ProQuest; accessed 8 September 2004.

[53]Brooke, A1.

[54]Gordon Fairclough, "Seoul Steps Up Push for Dealing with Pyongyang; South Korea Will Urge U.S. to Be More Flexible in Nuclear-Program Talks," *The Wall Street Journal*, (August 2004); [database on-line]; available from ProQuest; accessed 8 September 2004.

[55]Ibid.

[56]Ibid.

[57]Onishi, A1.

[58]Brooke, A1.

[59]Eve Conant, "Our Man In Libya?" *Newsweek*, (New York, 20 December 2004, p. E6); [database on-line]; available from ProQuest; accessed 9 March 2005.

[60]Fairclough, "Seoul Steps Up Push for Dealing with Pyongyang."

BIBLIOGRAPHY

Allison, Graham. "'94 Deal with North Korea Holds Lessons for Today." *The New York Times* (20 July 2004), p. E.6. Database on-line. Available from ProQuest. Accessed 31 August 2004.

Baker, James A. III. "Nuclear Pyongyang." *The Wall Street Journal*, (16 August 2004), p. A12. Database on-line. Available from ProQuest. Accessed 8 September 2004.

Boucher, Richard, U.S. Department of State – Press Statement, "Six-Party Talks on North Korean Nuclear Program." 28 February 2004 Available from <http://www.state.gov/r/pa/prs/ps/2004/29989.htm>. Internet. Accessed 19 December 2004.

Brodie, Bernard. *The Test of Korea," War and Politics.* New York: Macmillan Publishing Co, 1973.

Brooke, James. "Japanese Angry Over Korean Kidnappings." *The New York Times* 20 March 2002. Available from <http://www.freeserbia.net/Articles/2002/Kidnappings.html>. Internet. Accessed 19 December 2004.

_____. "2 Koreas Sidestep U.S. to Forge Pragmatic Links." *The New York Times*, (26 June 2004), p. A1. Database on-line. Available from ProQuest. Accessed 31 August 2004.

Bush, George W. *The National Security Strategy of the United States of America.* Washington, D.C.: The White House, September 2002.

Chenowith, Gregg and Tricia Miller. "A Heartless Homeland." *Christianity Today*, October 2004. Available from<http:// www.christianitytoday.com/ct/2004/010/29.45.html>. Internet. Accessed 26 October 2004.

"Committee on International Relations – Congressional Testimony, "U.S. House of Representatives, 24 September 1998." Available from <http://commdocs.house.gov/committees/intrel/hfa52334.000/hfa52334_0.htm>. Internet. Accessed 29 August 2004.

Conant, Eve. "Our Man In Libya?" *Newsweek*, (New York, 20 December 2004, p. E6); Database on-line. Available from ProQuest. Accessed 9 March 2005.

Country Watch. "North Korea - 2004 Country Review." Country Watch Reviews, 2004 Edition. Available from<http://www.countrywatch.com>. Internet. Accessed 8 August 2004.

Defense Intelligence Agency Report, "North Korea: The Foundations of Military Strength." October 1991, Available from<http://www.fas.org/irp/product/knfms/knfms_chp3.html>. Internet. Accessed 19 December 2004.

Ellings, Richard J., and Aaron L. Friedberg, eds. *Strategic Asia 2003-2004: Fragility and Crisis.* Seattle: National Bureau of Asian Research, 2003.

Fairclough, Gordon. "Seoul Steps Up Push for Dealing with Pyongyang; South Korea Will Urge U.S. to Be More Flexible in Nuclear-Program Talks." *The Wall Street Journal*,

(31 August 2004), p. A10. Database on-line. Available from ProQuest. Accessed 8 September 2004.

The Friends Committee on National Legislation (FCNL). "U.S. Policy Towards North Korea: An Overview," August 2003; Available from <http://www.fcnl.org/whatis.htm>. Internet. Accessed 29 August 2004.

Global Security.org. "Republic of Korea Military Guide, North and South Korea Military Comparison, 2002." Available from <http://www.paulnoll.com/Korea/History/Korean-military.html>. Internet. Accessed 26 September 2004.

Kerr, Paul. U.S. Unveils Offer at North Korea Talks. *Arms Control Today*, p. 35-37. July/August 2004.

Kim, Ah-Young. "Targeting Pyongyang's Drug Trade Addiction." *Asia Times On-Line*, (June 2003). Available from <http://www.atimes.com/atimes/Korea/EF18Dg02.html>. Internet. Accessed 7 November 2004.

Niksch, Larry A. "Korea: U.S. – Korean Issues for Congress," CRS Issue Brief for Congress, 18 July 2003. Available from <http://fas.org/man/crs/IB98045.pdf>. Internet. Accessed 18 January 2005.

Noland, Marcus. "North Korea and the South Korean Economy." Institute for International Economics, 24 February 2003, p.1. Available from<http://www.iie.com/publications/papers/noland0203.htm>. Internet. Accessed 23 January 2005.

"North Korea Won't Abandon Nuclear Programs, North Korea Says It Can't Abandon Nuclear Programs after South Korean Nuclear Experiments." *The Associated Press*, September 2004, ABCNews.com. Available from <http://printerfriendly.abcnews.com/printerfriendly/Print?fetchFromGLUE=true&GLUESer>. Internet. Accessed 5 October 2004.

Onishi, Norimitsu. "North Korea is Reaching Out, and World is Reaching Back." *The New York Times*, (20 August 2004), p. A1. Database on-line. available from ProQuest. Accessed September 2004.

ParaPundit. "On China's Aid to North Korea and Sanctions," 9 July 2003. Available from <http://www.parapundit.com/archives/001464.html>. Internet. Accessed 19 December 2004.

Rhem, Kathleen. "North Korean Military Very Credible Conventional Force." United States Department of Defense, American Forces Information Service News Articles, November 2003. Available from <http://www.defenselink.mil/news/Nov2003/n11182003_200311181.html>. Internet. Accessed 15 September 2004.

_____. "North Korea Intercepts Air Force Aircraft." Air Force Print News, American Forces Press Service, March 2003. Available from <http://www.af.mil/news/story_print.asp?storyID =30403665>. Internet. Accessed 8 December 2004.

Sanger, David E. "U.S. Persuades Allies to Halt North Korean Atom Project." *The New York Times*, (5 November 2003), p. A12. Database on-line. Available from ProQuest. Accessed 31 August 2004.

"Six Party Talks, U.S. Department of State Press Release." 2 March 2004. Available from <http://www.state.gov/p/eap/rls/rm/2004/30093.htm>. Internet. Accessed 23 January 2005.

U.S. Central Intelligence Agency, "The World Factbook, South Korea," 2003, p. 7-8; Available from <http://www.cia.gov/cia/publications/factbook/print/ks.html>. Internet. Accessed 23 January 2005.

U.S. Congress. House of Representatives. Committee on International Relations. "U.S. North Korean Policy," September 1998. Available from <http://commdocs.house.gov/committees /intrel/hfa52334.000/hfa52334_0.htm>. Internet. Accessed 29 August 2004.

U.S.S. Pueblo Exhibit, National Security Agency Museum. Available from <http://www.nsa.gov /museum/museu00032.cfm>. Internet. Accessed 8 December 2004.

www.ingramcontent.com/pod-product-compliance
Lightning Source LLC
Chambersburg PA
CBHW081812280526
45789CB00008B/3109